THE FRIDAY

HARVEST

A Guide to Growing Wealth Through Weekly Options

JAROH SLAYDEN

TABLE OF CONTENTS

INTRODUCTION

We frequently seek a guiding star—a light that illuminates a road to financial freedom—in the wide expanse of the financial world, where aspirations of money and success dance like faraway stars. A lesser-known, yet spectacular, point of light occurs inside this heavenly journey—weekly options trading. Imagine a world where every Friday isn't only the start of the weekend, but also the start of your paycheck, and your financial efforts bore fruit like a bountiful crop.

As another week comes to an end, there's a certain exhilaration in knowing that the next Friday may provide more than simply the promise of leisure. It carries the potential of wealth, which is created by the skill of trading weekly options. This book, "The Friday Harvest," will help you comprehend, embrace, and dominate this thrilling arena of financial possibility.

Consider this: you, the astute investor, are standing on the outskirts of a vast, fruitful field. It stretches out in front of you, brimming with possibilities. Each week, you sow the seeds of knowledge and strategy, and as Friday comes, you look forward to reaping the benefits. Although the premise is simple—trading options with shorter time horizons—the ramifications for your financial future are deep.

"The Friday Harvest" takes you on a tour across this financial terrain to help you develop your wealth, regardless of your level of experience. Whether you are a seasoned trader or new to the world of options, this book provides the tools, methods, and insights you need to make Fridays more than just the conclusion of the workweek— they become the precursor to your own financial harvest.

Within these pages, you will learn about the complexities of weekly options, including their profit potential and unique ability to react to an ever-changing financial environment. We'll look at ways for increasing your profits while handling hazards with confidence. Even in the face of uncertainty, you will learn to manage your investments with discipline and understanding.

"The Friday Harvest" is a tapestry of events as well as a voyage of knowledge. Real-life case studies will take you through the ups and downs of other traders' careers, providing you with priceless lessons and insights. Each narrative demonstrates the practical use of weekly options and the opportunities they bring.

This book isn't just about Fridays; it's about creating a long-term and expanding stream of income. We'll look at the power of weekly options to learn about compound interest, long-term wealth development, and even retirement planning.

So, whether you're looking for financial stability, adventure, or simply want to learn more about the world of options trading, "The Friday Harvest" invites you to join us on this fascinating trip. Together, we will open the door to a future in which each Friday marks the start of your own personal payday—a harvest of riches, opportunity, and financial progress.

Prepare to discover, learn, and prosper as we sail the oceans of weekly possibilities, where your financial future is just one transaction away. Hello and welcome to "The Friday Harvest."

CHAPTER 1
COMPREHENDING WEEKLY OPTIONS

There are several tactics and instruments available in the realm of finance and investing to assist individuals in increasing their wealth. Options trading stands out as a potent instrument for both experienced and inexperienced investors. Options allow you to harness the fluctuations of financial markets and use them to your advantage. Weekly options have evolved as an intriguing and dynamic technique to possibly expand your investing portfolio inside the world of options.

This chapter looks into the principles of weekly options, laying the groundwork for a trip into the core of wealth creation using this powerful financial tool. We'll delve into the complexities of options trading and cover the unique traits that make weekly options an appealing alternative.

Investigating Weekly Options

Weekly options have arisen as a light of potential for traders seeking quick, high-frequency techniques in the ever-changing environment of financial markets, where chances can flash by in the blink of an eye. Imagine a world in which you don't have to wait a month to reap the results of your labour; a future in which you may grab control of your financial destiny every seven days.

The introduction of weekly options changed the way traders approached the financial markets. Unlike their regular monthly cousins, which have a longer lifespan, weekly options provide an appealing proposition: the opportunity to profit from price swings in a short period of time. This financial breakthrough ushers in a new era of agility and flexibility in response to the increased need for faster trading possibilities.

The sheer flexibility that weekly alternatives provide is at the heart of their appeal. By shortening the expiry period from a month to a week, traders have unprecedented flexibility in tailoring their positions to various market situations and capitalising on short-term trading opportunities. Weekly options may be your trusty friend whether you're an enthusiastic day trader hunting for fast winnings or an investor trying to properly manage risk.

Weekly options are not restricted to a particular asset class or investment type. They are available for a wide variety of financial assets such as equities, exchange-traded funds (ETFs), and indexes. Because of their versatility, they are a helpful tool for both new and experienced traders. Weekly options give a broad canvas on which to paint your financial plans, whether you want to create continuous income, preserve your existing holdings, or speculate on short-term price swings.

The trading frequency of weekly options is one of its important characteristics. The shorter expiry term encourages greater market participation. It enables you to quickly change your portfolio to changing market circumstances and capitalise on emerging possibilities. Weekly options allow you to conduct additional trades, fine-tune your methods, and remain ahead of the curve.

While the prospect of rapid gains and high-frequency trading is clearly tempting, it is not without its own set of difficulties. Because weekly alternatives have a faster temporal decay, every decision is more important. The importance of risk management and discipline cannot be overstated. Weekly options, with the correct methods and a clear grasp of the dangers, may be a dynamic instrument for generating wealth.

Exploring weekly choices is like beginning on a great financial trip. It's a voyage through uncertain markets, adapting to ever-changing conditions, and harnessing the potential for quick development. We will go deeper into the subtleties of weekly options in the next chapters, from contract specifications to trading methods, risk management, and real-life case studies. Through "The Friday Harvest," we will unleash the magic of short-term earnings and guide you to financial success. So buckle up and prepare for an exciting voyage into the world of weekly alternatives. Your financial fate is waiting for you.

Weekly Option Benefits and Risks

No investment opportunity is without pros and disadvantages. This section will go over the advantages of weekly options, such as flexibility, increased trading chances, and the possibility for faster gains.

Here are several advantages of using weekly options into your investment strategy:

Flexibility: Weekly options provide traders with the flexibility to adjust to quickly changing market conditions. With seven-day expirations, you may swiftly modify your holdings to capitalise on short-term opportunities.

Higher Profit Potential: The weekly options' reduced time frame offers for the possibility of faster earnings. Traders can capture market swings in a shorter time frame, perhaps resulting in more frequent profits.

Reduced Capital Commitment: When compared to standard monthly options, weekly options often demand less capital. This implies you may invest less and diversify your portfolio more efficiently.

Diversification: You may diversify your trading strategy by using weekly options. You can trade many options at the same time, spreading your risk over multiple assets or methods.

Hedging Opportunities: Weekly options may be used to hedge and protect current holdings in your portfolio. You can use them to reduce losses or protect your investments from bad market swings.

Enhanced Liquidity: Many weekly options have strong trading volumes and liquidity due to their popularity. This liquidity assures narrow bid-ask spreads, lowering trading costs and enabling quick executions.

Reduced Time Decay: Because weekly options have a shorter expiry duration, time decay (theta decay) is less evident compared to monthly options. This might be advantageous while managing your positions.

Weekly options are popular among income-seeking traders because they generate consistent income. Through methods like as covered calls and cash-secured puts, they can provide constant revenue, allowing you to benefit on a regular basis.

Adaptability to News Events: Weekly options are ideal for traders who wish to react to news and events as quickly as possible. Earnings reports, economic data releases, and geopolitical developments may all be used to position your portfolio.

Learning Opportunities: Participating in weekly activities provides a rich learning experience. Trading more often helps you to obtain hands-on experience, hone your trading abilities, and gain a deeper understanding of market dynamics.

Weekly options may be used strategically to target specific price moves, making them ideal for swing trading and capitalising on short-term trends.

You may access these benefits and establish a dynamic and adaptive investing programme that corresponds with your financial goals and risk tolerance by investigating weekly possibilities. However, it is critical to note that weekly options carry additional risks, and success requires a solid grasp of the market as well as good risk management.

Weekly Options Risks

Weekly options can be extremely susceptible to short-term price swings and market volatility. Price swings that are sudden and rapid might result in big profits or losses in a short period of time.

Time Decay: Because weekly options have a shorter time horizon, time decay (theta) can destroy the option's value more quickly. If the underlying asset does not move as predicted, time decay can cause severe losses.

With only a one-week expiration term, there is little time to make modifications to your holdings if they move against you. If the market moves in an unfavourable direction, this lack of flexibility may result in higher losses.

Greater Transaction Costs: Trading weekly options more frequently may result in greater transaction costs, such as fees and bid-ask spreads, which can eat into your earnings.

Weekend market gaps can have a significant impact on weekly options. If the market starts much higher or lower than the previous close, option holders may suffer surprise losses.

Overtrading Risk: The allure of rapid profits in weekly options can lead to overtrading, in which investors take unwarranted risks or trade too frequently, potentially resulting in losses.

Emotional Stress: The fast pace of weekly option trading can be emotionally stressful. Poor trading outcomes might stem from emotional decision-making, such as panic selling or hasty purchasing.

Weekly options frequently necessitate a more concentrated concentration on a few select assets, reducing your capacity to diversify your portfolio efficiently.

Lack of previous Data: When compared to regular monthly options, weekly options may not have as much previous data accessible for study. This can make developing educated trading strategies more difficult.

Assignment Risk: If you are a seller of weekly options, you face the risk of early assignment, which requires you to receive or deliver the underlying asset sooner than intended, possibly disrupting your trading strategy.

Weekly options can be more difficult to trade and comprehend, especially for new investors. Before trading weekly options, it's critical to understand the fundamentals of options trading.

To reduce these risks, it's critical to have a well-thought-out trading plan, put risk management methods in place, and constantly educate yourself on options trading. When considering weekly alternatives, you can only make educated judgements if you fully grasp the hazards involved.

CHAPTER 2
LAYING THE GROUNDWORK FOR SUCCESS

Every trip in the magnificent tapestry of financial success begins with a vision, a strategy, and a willingness to shoot for the skies. "Laying the Groundwork for Success" is your guidebook for this incredible journey into the world of weekly options trading. It's the chapter where you establish the groundwork for your financial future, armed with the tools and information needed to navigate the market's unpredictability.

Setting Specific Financial Objectives

The path to financial success begins with a clear sense of purpose. There are threads in the enormous fabric of life that glitter with meaning and illuminate our road to greatness. None of these shine as brightly as the financial objectives we establish for ourselves. Setting specific financial objectives is comparable to creating a road map to your future, a strong expression of will to live the life you want. It is an art and a science, a vision and a plan intertwined to guide you to the treasure troves of prosperity and fulfilment.

The deep insight that your intentions influence your reality is at the heart of financial goal setting. When you create specific financial objectives, you give your ambitions new life. Your objectives become a road plan, directing your activities and adding meaning into your financial path. Setting goals is more than just wishful thinking; it is a complex psychological and physiological process. When you present your brain with a clear aim, it mobilises your inner resources, boosts motivation, and concentrates your activities with unflinching commitment.

Consider yourself at the helm of a ship, looking out into the huge, unknown sea of your financial destiny. This is where you create your vision statement, a beacon that will guide you through stormy seas and sunny days. It is your unshakeable dedication to a desired future that guides your financial ship. Financial objectives, like stars in the night sky, come in a variety of shapes and sizes. You have short-term ambitions that flash over the sky in flashes of brilliance, like meteors. Mid-term objectives are like planets that are visible for extended periods of time, while long-term goals are like constellations that form the backdrop of your life's financial tale.

The SMART strategy - *Specific, Measurable, Achievable, Relevant, and Time-Bound* - is required to define clear financial goals. It's the same as assigning each star in the sky a name, position, brightness, and time of appearance. This method takes your ideas and turns them into a tangible strategy. Goals are the destinations on your financial plan, but getting there requires a road map. Your roadmap is your action plan, a set of steps that will get you closer to your goal. It's a comprehensive map that shows you the best path to your riches.

The road to financial success is not without difficulties. Fear, doubt, outside demands, and diversions may all cloud your judgement. Understanding these roadblocks and understanding how to overcome them is a critical component of the process. Milestones are financial rest spots, where you may relax and refresh. They remind you of how far you've gone, urging you ahead with newfound zeal. Every minor victory demonstrates your perseverance and growth. Your financial journey is an adventure, and it, like all trips, will alter. Being adaptable, altering your route as needed, and grabbing unexpected chances are all important abilities to have on your financial journey. Setting specific financial objectives entails accepting your financial fate. It is a matter of proclaiming your intentions to the universe and committing to a path of riches and fulfilment. It's about realising that you are the creator of your own tale, and that by setting specific objectives, you are creating a masterpiece that will brighten your life and the lives of people around you. So, embrace the power of clarity, create goals, and begin out on a path to financial plenty. Your fate is waiting for you, and you are the captain of your financial ship, charting a route to a happier and more wealthy future.

Risk Tolerance Evaluation

Just as no two traders are the same, no two risk tolerances are the same. Understanding your risk tolerance is the North Star that leads your trip in the complicated world of financial decision-making. A knowledgeable investor must measure their risk tolerance to traverse the world of finance, much as an explorer designs a path based on the terrain they can overcome. This is where the skill of assessing risk tolerance comes into play.

Consider risk tolerance assessment to be a compass that guides you through the maze of financial possibilities. It's a skill that blends self-reflection, financial knowledge, and emotional intelligence. Risk tolerance is your umbrella in a world where financial decisions may be as unpredictable as the weather. Risk is a range of possibilities, not a single force. Each person's risk tolerance is like a distinct brushstroke on a canvas. Some investors may be willing to take on high-risk, high-reward investments, while others prefer the security of low-risk, stable assets. Your risk profile is your colour palette, expressing your financial goals and concerns. Your risk tolerance is more than just a number; it reflects your emotional landscape. The excitement of a possible windfall, the fear of a market meltdown, and the joy of consistent, incremental gains all add to your financial picture. Understanding the psychology of your financial decisions is an important element of the evaluation process.

Just like an artist needs tools to make a masterpiece, analysing your risk tolerance necessitates the use of tools such as questionnaires and surveys. These tools probe your psychology, asking pertinent questions to ascertain your financial temperament. Balancing your risk tolerance with your financial goals is like to forging a journey through new territory. If your goal is to preserve your money, you may want to take a more conservative, steady approach. If wealth building is your aim, you may want to steer clear of riskier, possibly high-reward investments. Your investing decisions are the ship that will take you to your financial destination. Risk tolerance is the point at which fantasies and realities collide. It is the moment at which your financial objectives coincide with your readiness to withstand swings, disappointments, and market volatility. Here you will discover the actual route to financial success, where your goals will not be hampered by illogical concerns or excessive greed.

Mastering the art of risk tolerance assessment reveals the power of self-awareness. It gives you the ability to make informed financial decisions that align with your beliefs, ambitions, and temperament. It enables you to manage the volatile financial world with grace, intelligence, and assurance. Understanding your risk tolerance is like to carrying a reliable compass in your pocket. It guarantees that you stick to your financial plan, adjust to the ever-changing environment, and achieve your goals. Accept risk tolerance assessment as an art form, and you'll find yourself fearlessly creating your financial masterpiece, one bold brushstroke at a time.

Making a Trading Strategy

A ship adrift is adrift, and a trader adrift is lost in the financial wilderness. A trading strategy serves as a lighthouse illuminating your way in the frenetic arena of financial markets, where fortunes are earned and lost with the rise and fall of stock prices. It's more than just a piece of paper; it's your road map to financial success. Here, we look at the art of creating a trading plan, which is your key to navigating the complex world of trading with ability and strategy. A trading strategy is the foundation of your trading adventure. It's the blueprint that lays out your goals, methods, and regulations. From seasoned experts to newbies, every trader relies on a well-structured plan to lead them through the difficult maze of trading. Your trading strategy should begin with clear and explicit goals. What do you want to accomplish by trading? Are you seeking for consistent income, to build wealth, or to hedge your investments? Your goals serve as the North Star that guides your trading selections.

An effective trading strategy must be detailed in your trading plan. Will you be a day trader, a swing trader, or an investor for the long term? Each strategy has its own set of tactics, and your plan should give a clear guidance on which methods to employ. Your plan should outline the factors that will cause you to enter a trade as well as your exit strategy. Setting stop-loss orders to minimise prospective losses and take-profit orders to safeguard your winnings are examples of this. Clear guidelines for entering and leaving transactions promote discipline while reducing emotional decision-making. Effective risk management is a critical component of any trading strategy. A vital part is position sizing, or deciding the size of your transactions in relation to your capital. Managing risk on each trade is critical for protecting your wealth and ensuring market longevity. Mechanisms for continual monitoring and assessment should be included in your trading strategy. Examine your trading performance on a regular basis, scrutinise your judgements, and learn from your mistakes. This self-reflection process helps you to adjust and develop your trading strategy as you go. Trading may be an emotionally draining experience. Your strategy should cover the psychological components of trading, teaching you how to handle stress, maintain discipline, and avoid making rash judgements in stressful situations. Even the best-laid plans sometimes run across unexpected roadblocks. Your strategy should include contingency plans for various eventualities, ensuring you're ready to deal with unfavourable market circumstances or unforeseen occurrences.

A well-structured trading strategy is more than simply a piece of paper in the trading industry; it's your own ideology. It represents your dedication to trade in a disciplined, knowledgeable, and strategic manner. Creating a trading plan is more than simply creating a paper; it is also about creating a financial strategy, a game plan, and a route to success. With your trading strategy as your guide, you will begin your trading experience with confidence, armed with the information and tactics to manage the market's intricacies. It's more than simply a strategy; it's your ticket to the world of trading, where you may execute your ideas with accuracy and maximise your financial potential.

Creating a Solid Foundation

Weekly options trading success is built on a solid basis. The humble hero is a sturdy foundation, the basis upon which lofty feats are constructed. Your route to success in any endeavour involves the creation of a firm foundation, just as an architect meticulously sets the foundations for a spectacular skyscraper. Let's look at how to lay the groundwork for your goals, whether they be in business, education, personal growth, or anything else. A solid foundation is not a one-size-fits-all notion; it is tailored to the unique requirements of your objectives. Consider it a custom-made outfit, tailored to offer the precise support and stability needed for your voyage. The foundation of your success is a purposeful combination of information, skills, mentality, and resources. Education is frequently the first brick laid in your foundation. Knowledge is the foundation of any successful journey, whether you choose conventional education, online courses, or self-directed study. It gives you the tools you need to face difficulties, make educated decisions, and innovate. Your foundation's building bricks are your skills. Each talent adds to your capacity to flourish in your chosen career, from communication and problem-solving to technical proficiency and critical thinking. You construct your skill set layer by layer, much like a mason building a wall.

A solid foundation is made up of both tangible and intangible elements. Your mental outlook, beliefs, and attitudes establish the foundation for your success. The steel girders that reinforce your foundation are a growth mindset, resilience, and a positive attitude. Wise resource management is like the cement that holds your foundation together. Financial knowledge, time management, and organisational abilities are required for effective resource management. The more efficiently you manage your resources, the more stable and resilient your foundation will be. Your foundation's support system is its network of relationships. Your relationships, like pillars, supply you with direction, mentorship, cooperation chances, and emotional support. It is critical to establish and maintain a strong network. A solid foundation is not static; it must be maintained on an ongoing basis. Self-care, which includes physical health, mental well-being, and work-life balance, serves as your foundation's maintenance crew. Taking care of your physical and emotional needs on a regular basis ensures that your foundation remains strong.

Adaptability is like the flexible joints of a construction in today's fast-paced environment. It enables your foundation to absorb shocks, pivot as needed, and develop as conditions change. The capacity to adapt is essential for building a solid foundation. A solid foundation is more than the sum of its components; it serves as your springboard to success. It gives you the stability you need to weather storms, the information you need to make educated decisions, and the support you need to conquer challenges. Whether you're starting a business, pursuing a profession, or seeking personal development, keep in mind that a firm foundation is the cornerstone upon which your dreams will soar. With the proper foundation, your trip will reach new heights.

CHAPTER 3
BASICS OF WEEKLY OPTIONS

Timing is essential in the fast-paced world of financial markets. Weekly options are dynamic and adaptable instruments that capture the essence of time, allowing traders to profit from market changes over a shorter time frame. This weekly option fundamentals examination will teach you the main ideas that drive these products and how they may become a vital element of your trading approach.

Consider classic options to be the trading world's marathon runners, striving for a far finish line. Weekly options, on the other hand, are sprinters, covering a shorter distance in a shorter period of time. These options, as the name implies, expire weekly, providing traders with a shortened and concentrated window for their strategy.

Weekly vs. Monthly Options: A Timeline Battle

Weekly options and its elder, more traditional sister, monthly options, take centre stage in the broad arena of options trading. The speed and agility of weekly alternatives are pitted against the endurance and stability of monthly options in this temporal fight. Let's look at the rivalry between these two and see when and why each deserves a spot in your trading plan.

The Need for Speed: Weekly Alternatives

First round: agility

Weekly options emerged as the sprinters of the options industry. These contracts have weekly expirations and have a relatively small time horizon. This agility is perfect for traders who want immediate returns and are willing to make shorter-term commitments.

Round 2: Adaptability

Consider having the freedom to create a fresh option strategy every week. Weekly choices are available. They enable traders to fine-tune their strategies and adapt precisely to quickly changing market conditions.

Round 3: Rapid Results

One of the most major advantages of weekly options is the possibility of making money faster. The compressed period allows traders to capitalise on chances and earn higher returns on their investments, which may be quite enticing to people who thrive on short-term earnings.

Tradition's Stability: Monthly Options

Endurance is the first round.

Monthly options are the possibilities world's marathon runners. They give a more steady and lengthier time period for trading, with expirations generally at the end of each month. Long-term investors and those seeking stability will benefit from this durability.

Round 2: Volume and Liquidity

Monthly options often have better liquidity and trading volume. Because of the popularity of these options, traders may find it simpler to initiate and exit positions with narrow bid-ask spreads.

Round 3: Predictability and Planning

Traders have more time to design and implement their tactics with a monthly schedule. It provides for a more cautious approach, allowing investors to evaluate market patterns and have a longer-term perspective.

When Should You Choose Which?

There is no apparent winner in the battle between weekly and monthly alternatives. It's more about selecting the proper instrument for the job.

Select Weekly Options when;

- You thrive on fast-paced trading and are looking for rapid profits.
- You want the ability to quickly adjust to shifting market conditions.
- You're okay with a higher level of risk and volatility.
- You are an aggressive trader who appreciates the challenge of trading in the short term.

Select Monthly Options when;

- You want a longer investing horizon and seek steadiness.
- You appreciate liquidity and want to be able to enter and exit positions with ease.
- You prefer a more measured trading technique, with time for in-depth study.
- You are a long-term investor or like to "set and forget" your investments.

The true winners in the battle of weekly options vs. monthly options are those who understand when to use both in their trading approach. These two periods work well together, providing traders with a varied arsenal for adapting to changing market conditions and individual preferences. The secret to success is not to favour one over the other, but to understand when to take use of the agility of weekly options and when to take advantage of the endurance of monthly options. It's a dynamic duo that enables traders to manoeuvre through the ever-changing world of finance with precision and strategy.

In the world of trading, time is frequently crucial to success. Weekly options, with their shorter expiration term, present a distinct mix of benefits and risks. Understanding the fundamentals of weekly options is the first step towards incorporating time into your trading strategy. Weekly options are a crucial instrument to consider in your financial path, whether you're a seasoned trader searching for nimble chances or a newbie eager to explore the world of options.

Expiration Dates and Strike Prices

Strike prices and expiration dates act as the compass and the clock of your financial journey. They are the two pillars that underpin the sophisticated architecture of options contracts, allowing traders to accurately specify their tactics and traverse the always ticking clock of market dynamics. Let's look at the beauty and relevance of strike prices and expiry dates, which are the foundations of option trading.

The Precise Aim of Strike Prices

The sharpshooter's crosshairs are strike prices, which identify the price at which an options contract permits the holder to purchase or sell the underlying asset. They are an important component of options contracts because they allow traders to establish exact entry and exit points for their holdings. Strike prices are available in a variety of options, giving traders the accuracy they need to fit their tactics with market circumstances and personal goals.

Choosing the optimal strike price is analogous to a craftsman picking the appropriate tool for the job at hand. It is determined by the trader's viewpoint and strategy:

At-the-Money (ATM): An ATM strike price is the closest to the underlying asset's current market price. It's a good option for traders who anticipate mild price fluctuation.

In-the-Money (ITM): strike prices are advantageous when traders want to execute the option right away. They already have inherent worth.

Out-of-the-Money (OTM) strike prices provide extra price movement power. They have no intrinsic worth and are often less expensive.

Choosing the proper strike price necessitates a thorough market research, a defined trading aim, and an evaluation of risk tolerance.

The Ticking Clock of Expiration Dates

The expiry date is the timer that counts down the life of an option contract. It denotes the moment at which the contract ceases to exist and is rendered worthless if not exercised. Different choices have different expiration periods, with some ending in days (weekly options) and others lasting months or even years.

Traders must be as accurate with their choice of expiration date as a skilled chef is with the timing of each dish:

Weekly Options: Weekly options have a short expiration date and are popular among traders aiming for rapid gains or reacting to certain news events.

Monthly Expirations: Because monthly options have a longer time horizon, they are appropriate for longer-term strategies such as hedging or income creation.

LEAPS (Long-Term Equity Anticipation Securities): LEAPS are designed for investors with long time horizons. They can be utilised for long-term investments or strategic positioning.

The expiration date should be chosen in accordance with your trading strategy and your expectations for the underlying asset's price movement.

Strike prices and expiry dates are not separate elements; they work together to create accurate and successful options trading strategies. The strike price and expiry date should be carefully considered in light of your market view, risk tolerance, and trading objectives. Strike prices and expiry dates are the conductor's baton and metronome in the symphony of options trading, ensuring that your trading methods are played with accuracy and time. They enable traders to fine-tune their positions and implement their plans with astounding precision. It's an art form that takes options trading from speculative to a measured and purposeful dance with the financial markets.

Put and Call Options

Call and put options are two fundamental tools in the volatile world of options trading. They are the yin and yang of the options universe, providing traders with separate and complimentary methods of capitalising on market fluctuations. Let's dig into the interesting and interrelated world of call and put options, which is rife with possibilities and tactics.

Call Options: A Route to Potential Gain

Call options are a financial tool that allows traders to speculate on the rise of an underlying asset, such as a stock, index, or commodity. A call option holder believes that the asset's price will climb before or by the contract's expiration, much like a hiker ascending a mountain route with the anticipation of reaching a summit. Call options are contracts that provide the holder the right, but not the duty, to purchase the underlying asset at a predetermined price known as the strike price. This price acts as a key to a treasure chest, opening the possibility of profit if the asset's market value surpasses the striking price. Call option traders (sometimes known as "call buyers") expect price increases. If the market price of the asset increases over the strike price, they can exercise their call options and purchase the asset at the lower strike price. This allows them to benefit from the differential between market and strike prices.

Put Options: A Protective Measure Against Market Downturns

Put options protect against market downturns. Put options allow traders to safeguard their assets in the same way that a prudent investor diversifies their portfolio to reduce risk. The right, but not the responsibility, to sell the underlying asset at a defined strike price is granted by put options. Put options are the preferred financial instrument for traders who predict a drop in the market value of an asset. Put buyers, like wary weather forecasters, brace themselves for a storm. If the market price of the asset falls below the strike price, they can exercise their put options and sell the asset at the higher strike price, earning from the difference.

The Interaction between Calls and Puts

The world of options trading is more than just picking sides. Indeed, traders frequently mix call and put options in a variety of ways to develop complex strategies that protect, hedge, or maximise their prospective returns. This interaction between calls and puts provides traders with a toolbox of options for aligning their positions with market dynamics and their own financial goals.

Covered Calls: A trading method in which a trader sells call options on an asset that they already own in order to generate revenue but restricting potential profit.

Protective Puts: A trading method in which a trader purchases put options to hedge an existing position against market downturns.

Straddles and strangles are strategies that include purchasing both call and put options on the same asset, allowing you to profit from substantial price swings in either direction. Call and put options are similar to dancing partners, with each taking turns leading and following. They allow traders to accept market volatility, whether rising to new heights or falling into uncertainty. Traders may wield call and put options with elegance and accuracy if they grasp the art and science of these instruments, designing strategies that correspond with their financial goals and risk tolerance. It's a dance of opportunity that allows traders to confidently and creatively traverse the volatile world of options trading.

Time and intrinsic value

These two aspects, like the yin and yang of options, work in tandem to define an options contract's price and potential. Let us investigate the unique interaction between intrinsic and temporal value and how it shapes the options market. Intrinsic value is the rock-solid underpinning of an options contract, indicating the option's tangible worth if exercised immediately. It is the price at which the option is "in-the-money," meaning it has actual value based on the underlying asset's current market price. The computation of intrinsic value is simple. It equals the market price of the underlying asset minus the strike price for a call option. It is the strike price minus the market price of the underlying asset for a put option. Simply put, intrinsic value is the amount of money you would receive if you exercised the option right now. In practise, the intrinsic value of an options contract may be transformed into actual profit by exercising the option. However, many options traders do not necessarily exercise options with intrinsic value; instead, they frequently elect to sell the option in order to benefit on its inherent value.

The mystery that surrounds options is time value, which represents the unpredictability and possibility for future price fluctuations. It is the fraction of an option's price that exceeds its intrinsic value, indicating the possibility that the option will grow more profitable with time. Time value, unlike intrinsic value, does not have a defined formula. It is impacted by a number of factors, including the period before the option expires, the implied volatility of the underlying asset, and the risk-free interest rate. As the expiry date approaches, time value falls, either eliminating totally at expiration (for out-of-the-money options) or changing into intrinsic value (for in-the-money options). Options traders frequently concentrate on tactics that leverage time value, whether by purchasing options with the hope of gaining time value as the market moves, or by selling options to catch time value decay. The speculative element of options trading comes to life with time value, which offers traders the possibility for big rewards as market dynamics develop. Options pricing is a delicate balance between intrinsic and time value. These parameters work together to calculate the total cost of an options contract. Options that are in the money have both intrinsic and temporal value, whereas options that are out of the money just have time value.

The two components that give life to options trading are intrinsic value and time value. They influence option pricing, methods, and potential, allowing traders to traverse the world of financial markets with accuracy and strategy. Traders may unlock the entire spectrum of options trading possibilities by grasping the fundamentals of intrinsic and time value, making educated judgements and capturing chances in a dynamic and ever-changing market. It's a symphony of financial potential in which traders may develop their own individual profit and strategy compositions.

CHAPTER 4

BEGINNING WITH WEEKLY OPTIONS

Weekly option trading success, like any other type of trading, is dependent on education and discipline. It is critical to educate yourself on a regular basis, maintain discipline in your approach, and successfully manage your risk. Weekly options are an exciting and dynamic way for traders to traverse the financial markets with speed and accuracy, but they can only be fully utilised with a well-informed and disciplined strategy. It's a thrilling trip, and with the correct preparation, the fast track to trading success is waiting.

Consider These Business Concepts

Firms that pay on a weekly basis are frequently associated with industries with regular cash flow, such as service-oriented firms, and frequently entail gig or freelance employment. Here are some company ideas that can produce revenue while also paying employees or contractors on a weekly basis:

Ridesharing or Food Delivery Services: Launch a ridesharing or food delivery business where drivers or couriers may earn money and get weekly rewards.

Freelance Services: Provide freelance services in a variety of industries, such as graphic design, writing, web development, or digital marketing, and get weekly payment for client projects.

Handyman or house Maintenance Services: Establish a firm that provides house repair, maintenance, or remodelling services, with contractors paid weekly.

Cleaning Services: Establish a cleaning business that offers home or commercial cleaning services and compensates employees or contractors on a weekly basis.

Event Planning: Provide wedding, party, or business event planning and coordinating services, compensating your event planners and assistants on a weekly basis.

Landscaping and Lawn Care Services: Establish a landscaping or lawn care company where employees or subcontractors can earn a weekly wage by maintaining outdoor environments.

Home Health Care Services: Create a home healthcare firm that offers in-home care for the elderly or those with special needs and pays carers on a weekly basis.

Short-Term Rentals: Invest in rental properties or provide short-term holiday rentals through platforms such as Airbnb to earn weekly rental revenue.

Fitness or Yoga Instruction: Become a certified fitness or yoga instructor and start teaching courses or providing personal training sessions. You can charge clients fees on a weekly basis.

Content Creation: Start a YouTube channel, blog, or podcast and monetize it with weekly ad income or sponsorships.

Dropshipping firm: Use a dropshipping model to start an e-commerce firm that sells things online without owning inventory and receives weekly income from sales.

Become a freelance photographer and offer photographic services for events, portraits, or commercial projects, collecting weekly income from customers.

Start a pet care business that includes pet sitting, dog walking, or pet boarding, and pay carers on a weekly basis.

Create a temporary staffing service that links businesses with temporary employees for short-term tasks and pays these individuals on a weekly basis.

Launch a mobile vehicle washing and detailing service and pay your team of car washes and detailers on a weekly basis.

Become a private instructor, giving your knowledge in various disciplines or talents in exchange for weekly fees from your pupils or their parents.

Provide virtual assistant services to entrepreneurs or small firms, such as email management, scheduling, or research, and charge customers on a weekly basis.

Online Courses: Create and sell online courses or webinars on sites like as Udemy or Teachable, and profit from course enrollments on a weekly basis.

Cleaning Product Sales: Sell cleaning items in a real store or on an e-commerce website to make weekly revenue.

Remember that company success typically depends on elements such as market demand, competition, your business plan, and your ability to produce exceptional products or services. Ensure that your financial management systems can handle weekly payments to workers or contractors.

The Value of Risk Management

Risk management is the art and science of recognising, analysing, and minimising possible hazards in order to safeguard and improve the well-being of an individual, organisation, or project. It is a vital part of decision-making and planning that is important in our personal and professional life. Let us look at the compelling importance of risk management and why it is a critical component of success. Risk management aids in the protection of assets, investments, and financial resources against possible losses. You want to protect your hard-earned money and resources, whether you're an individual investor, a business owner, or a project manager. You lower the possibility of financial losses by recognising and minimising risks.

Effective risk management helps decision-makers comprehend the potential repercussions of their actions. It enables people and organisations to make educated decisions by balancing expected advantages and potential hazards. This leads to more reasoned, considered decisions that are less likely to have unfavourable consequences. One of the fundamental goals of risk management is to reduce or eliminate losses. Organisations and individuals can take proactive efforts to reduce possible hazards by recognising them in advance. This might include putting in place safety precautions, making backup plans, or acquiring insurance, all of which decrease the financial and operational effect of unforeseen catastrophes.

In both the personal and professional arenas, reputation is priceless. Individuals and firms with effective risk management maintain their integrity and defend their reputation. Maintaining trust and credibility requires avoiding or efficiently dealing with catastrophes like as product recalls or data breaches. Many sectors and enterprises are subject to legal restrictions and compliance. Risk management assists an organisation in adhering to these requirements, avoiding costly penalties and legal challenges that may occur as a result of noncompliance.

Successful organisations are built to last. Long-term success requires the capacity to recognise and manage risks that might jeopardise an organization's or an individual's financial well-being. A well-structured risk management plan is a long-term investment. Risk management isn't only about preventing bad consequences; it may also encourage creativity and prudent risk-taking. Organisations and individuals may make educated decisions to seek new possibilities and enterprises by knowing possible risks. Risk management improves operational efficiency for firms by recognising possible obstacles and problems. It ensures that resources are used efficiently and that projects stay on track, avoiding costly delays. Preparing for crises is an important component of risk management. Having a well-thought-out risk management strategy in place ensures that organisations can respond efficiently and minimise disruption in the event of a natural disaster, a financial slump, or a worldwide pandemic. Peace of mind is provided by effective risk management. Knowing that possible risks have been analysed and mitigation procedures are in place helps individuals and organisations to focus on their goals with confidence and peace of mind.

Risk management is the hidden success hero. It's more than a precaution; it's a proactive approach that equips individuals and organisations with the knowledge and insight to negotiate the intricacies of life and business. By adopting risk management, we guarantee that our endeavours are safeguarded, our decisions are informed, and our future is more secure, resulting to better success and peace of mind in the long run.

Position Sizing Techniques

Position sizing is the process of selecting how much of a financial instrument (stocks, options, FX, and so on) to trade depending on your account size, risk tolerance, and trading strategy. It's all about finding the perfect mix of risk and profit. Position size is an important part of trading that frequently distinguishes successful traders from those who struggle to maintain consistency. It's not just about how much cash to put into a transaction; it's a comprehensive approach that protects your account, minimises risk, and maximises return potential. Let's take a look at position size tactics and see why they're so important in trading.

The main purpose of position sizing is to keep your trading capital safe. Traders are inevitably subjected to losing streaks and bad market circumstances. Position size correctly guarantees that a string of losses does not wreck your account and that you may continue trading during bad times. Position sizing has an impact on your capacity to capitalise on winning trades in addition to limiting losses. By effectively sizing positions, you ensure that profitable trades have a significant influence on your account balance.

Position size is critical in evaluating your trades' risk-to-reward ratio. It assists you in aligning your risk (the amount of money you're willing to lose) with your return (the profit possibility). A favourable risk-to-reward ratio is required for profitable trading. Your risk tolerance is a psychological and personal element. Effective position sizing takes into account your own risk tolerance. It enables you to establish boundaries that you are emotionally and financially ready to accept. Diversifying your portfolio is also part of position size. You spread risk by distributing funds to multiple transactions and asset types. This diversity can help preserve your wealth while also providing profit chances in a variety of market scenarios. Market circumstances can fluctuate quickly, and good position sizing responds to these changes. To limit risk, you may lower the size of your holdings in extremely volatile markets, whilst in stable markets, you may raise position sizes to capitalise on possible trends.

Some traders utilise the Kelly Criterion as a mathematical technique to identify optimal position sizing. It considers your trading strategy's advantage, your chances of success, and your bankroll. While it might be complicated, it provides a methodical approach to position sizing. Position sizing techniques are not fixed. Your approach to position sizing should develop as you learn and adjust. To accommodate changes in your trading strategy and market conditions, it is critical to analyse and modify your tactics. Position size tactics are the cornerstone of successful trading. Risk management, capital preservation, and profit maximisation are all part of it. Effective position size protects your money during difficult periods and helps you to profit from winning transactions. It is the foundation of trading prudence, allowing traders to confidently and precisely traverse the complexity of financial markets. Understanding and using position size tactics is critical to long-term trading success, whether you are a rookie or an experienced trader.

Asset Allocation and Diversification

With their accelerated timescales and dynamic character, weekly options provide a unique stage for the symphony of diversification and asset allocation to perform. These two concepts are critical in short-term trading because they orchestrate financial harmony, protect money, and pursue profit. Let's look at this amazing composition in the perspective of weekly alternatives. Weekly option diversification entails spreading your trading money over a range of underlying assets, such as individual stocks, indices, or ETFs. Diversification, like an orchestra, incorporates numerous instruments such as strings, brass, and woodwinds to build a balanced and resilient portfolio. The basic function of diversification is to decrease risk. Diversifying your bets across numerous assets helps lessen the impact of unfavourable market moves on your entire portfolio while trading weekly options, when the pace may be hectic. It's similar to composing a harmonic piece in which the tones compliment each other, eliminating dissonance.

Diversification isn't just about risk reduction, as previously said; it's also about capitalising on possibilities in the weekly options market. In various weeks, different assets or sectors may do well. By diversifying, you position yourself to capitalise on the qualities of each asset when they are at their peak, resulting in a financial composition that is both dynamic and adaptive. Weekly option asset allocation is like to a conductor directing an orchestra. It entails calculating how much cash to deploy to various assets or strategies depending on your financial objectives, risk tolerance, and market forecast. The rhythm of your trading strategy is established by this composition. In weekly options, asset allocation determines the balance of risk and return. Asset allocation establishes the balance of high-risk, high-reward positions and low-risk, stable holdings in your portfolio, much like a conductor adjusts the tempo for different parts of a symphony.

Asset distribution, like a conductor ensuring that each section of the symphony is in tune, needs frequent modifications. As market circumstances change, you may need to rebalance your weekly options portfolio to preserve your preferred asset mix. Weekly option asset allocation emphasises the long-term harmony of your trading approach. Rather than following short-term market noise, it focuses on orchestrating a symphony of transactions that can endure market volatility, resulting in long-term financial performance. Diversification and asset allocation work together to help you achieve your trading goals in the grand finale of your weekly options symphony. They ensure that your weekly options trading composition is strong and tailored to your specific needs.

Whether you're putting together a weekly options portfolio for income generation, hedging, or speculative trading, the combination of diversity and asset allocation is a fantastic path towards trading prudence. They lead you through the quick peaks and valleys of weekly options, providing a symphony of risk management and profit potential that aligns with your trading objectives. Diversification and asset allocation are your keys to weekly options composition in the realm of short-term trading, where every week offers a fresh overture, allowing you to execute an outstanding and strategic financial performance. Diversification and asset allocation are ideas in finance that are analogous to a harmonic symphony, where several instruments join together to create a masterpiece. These principles serve as the foundation for responsible investment, guiding people and organisations on a path to financial stability and success.

Contingency Plan

A contingency plan is a planned approach for dealing with unanticipated occurrences and obstacles. It lays out a clear plan for coping with unanticipated market moves, news events, and other variables that might effect your trades in the context of weekly options trading. In the realm of weekly options trading, where market circumstances may shift in the blink of an eye, having a well-thought-out contingency plan is like having a reliable compass to navigate you through choppy seas. This strategy is your lifeline in the case of an unforeseen incident or market instability. One of the primary goals of weekly options trading contingency planning is to anticipate and prepare for market volatility. Markets may be volatile, and unexpected price fluctuations or news might take traders off guard. A well-thought-out contingency plan can help you prepare for these events. Risk management is fundamental to contingency planning. It details how you will safeguard your capital and prevent potential losses in the event of a market downturn. It protects your trading account by implementing planned exit points and position-sizing techniques.

Markets are dynamic, and so should your trading technique. Contingency planning allows you to adapt your trading strategy in response to the ever-changing market environment. A contingency plan keeps you flexible and adaptive, whether it's moving from bullish to bearish positions or abandoning a transaction earlier than intended. Emotional decision-making is reduced by contingency planning. It enables you to rely on a set of pre-established norms and principles rather than making rash decisions in the heat of the moment. Emotion-driven trading can result in big losses, and contingency planning acts as a deterrent to such behaviour. Contingency plans do not come in one size fits all. They should be customised to your trading style, goals, and risk tolerance. Responses to events such as unexpected market collapses, big news releases, or technical analysis patterns that generate buy or sell signals might be part of your strategy. Stop-loss orders, profit-taking targets, position-sizing procedures, and predefined entry and exit locations are all common components of a solid contingency strategy. These elements serve as the instruments in your symphony, assisting you in maintaining harmony in your trade. Your backup plan is not static. After each trading experience, analyse how well your plan performed and make any required changes. Traders fine-tune their contingency plans for greater performance in the same way that a conductor fine-tunes their orchestra. A well-structured contingency strategy guarantees that you traverse the tumultuous seas of weekly options trading with confidence. It's your musical score, giving you structure and direction to help you adapt and prosper in the face of hardship. Contingency planning in weekly options trading is your trading prudence guardian in a world of market volatility and financial storms. It gives you the ability to meet unexpected situations with elegance and resilience, resulting in improved risk management and more confident trading judgements.

CHAPTER 5

LEARNING AND IMPROVEMENT ONGOING

Personal and professional growth is an ever-evolving process in a fast changing environment, much like a meandering river carving its way across new landscapes. The guiding concepts on this path are continuous learning and growth, which enable individuals to adapt, evolve, and eventually achieve in both their personal and professional life. The growth mindset, the concept that talents and intellect can be developed over time, is at the basis of continual learning and progress. Individuals who adopt this perspective recognise that obstacles and setbacks are chances for progress rather than constraints. Staying current in a world of fast-paced technology breakthroughs and evolving sectors is critical. Continuous learning ensures that you have the information and skills necessary to prosper in your chosen industry. The only constant in life is change. Learning and improvement allow you to more successfully adapt to changes in your work, personal life, or the world at large.

Learning is a never-ending adventure. It helps you to broaden your knowledge, experiment with new ideas, and get a better awareness of your surroundings. Continuous learning is what drives innovation and creativity. As you gain knowledge and experience, you will be better able to produce fresh ideas and solutions to challenging challenges. Continuous learning is a certain technique for career-minded individuals to ascend the professional ladder. Improvement can lead to promotions and possibilities for growth, whether through certifications, courses, or on-the-job experience. Learning and growth help you reduce hazards in both your personal and professional lives. You are more equipped to deal with unanticipated difficulties and failures. Learning is about more than simply professional progress; it is also about personal growth and fulfilment. It broadens your horizons, expands your worldview, and enhances your life. As you study and grow, you form relationships with like-minded people and professionals in your industry. These networks can lead to partnerships and possibilities that you would not have discovered otherwise. Continuous learning helps to build resilience. It gives you the mental and emotional tools you need to deal with life's ups and downs with grace and drive. You are more likely to create and achieve objectives if you are committed to continuous development. Every step forward is a success that brings you closer to your goals.

Learning and self-improvement strengthen your ability to lead and influence others. Others are drawn to people who are devoted to personal and professional development, whether in the job or in the community. As you continue to learn and grow, you not only benefit yourself but also contribute to the overall improvement of society. Your knowledge, creativity, and ideas may have a good influence on others and the world around you. The quest of constant learning and progress is, in essence, a lifetime adventure. It's an adventure that teaches people how to adapt, invent, succeed, and eventually prosper in an ever-changing environment. It is the river that carves its way across life's landscapes, leaving a legacy of development, achievement, and personal and professional success in its wake.

Making Mistakes and Learning from Them

Mistakes, while frequently undesired and unpleasant, are vital crucibles of growth and achievement. They are the foundations of wisdom and the driving forces behind personal and professional progress. Learning from errors not only helps people avoid repeating them, but it also serves as a foundation for resilience and a route to achievement. Accepting and owning mistakes is the first step in learning from them. Refusing to admit mistakes or blaming external forces might stifle progress. Accepting responsibility is an important step in the learning process. To get insights from mistakes, it is necessary to delve deeper and comprehend the underlying reasons. Was it a lack of information, a defective method, or a lapse of judgement? You may avoid making similar mistakes in the future by understanding the underlying causes.

Mistakes give an opportunity to change direction. They enable people to rethink their tactics and techniques. Those who learn from their errors have the capacity to adapt and make required changes. Resilience is defined as the ability to recover from hardship, and learning from mistakes promotes resilience. It improves problem-solving abilities and prepares people to meet problems with confidence and drive. Mistakes act as guideposts for continued progress. They highlight areas that require improvement and provide opportunity for advancement. Individuals become better versions of themselves by tackling these issues. Mistakes frequently result in a wealth of information and experience. They provide knowledge that is difficult to forget, and this knowledge becomes a useful asset for future endeavours. Errors humble people and remind them of their humanity. They also foster a growth mentality, in which obstacles and setbacks are viewed as chances for progress rather than restrictions.

Some of the most significant discoveries and creative breakthroughs have their origins in errors. The courage to explore, fail, and learn from those failures can lead to revolutionary breakthroughs. Individuals improve their decision-making processes by reflecting on prior mistakes. They become more discriminating, wise, and capable of making sound decisions. Making errors directly builds empathy and compassion for those facing similar circumstances. It has the potential to make people more sympathetic and helpful. The insight learned from making errors is frequently shared with others. Individuals contribute to communal knowledge and societal evolution by sharing their thoughts.

Overcoming failures increases motivation and persistence. It demonstrates that setbacks are fleeting and that individuals may accomplish their goals with perseverance. Leaders who freely admit and learn from their errors frequently obtain the respect and trust of their teams. It indicates sincerity and a desire to improve. Learning from errors is an essential component of personal and professional development. Mistakes are not failures; they are stepping stones to achievement. They build resilience, give knowledge, and motivate people to attain their best potential. Individuals may convert problems into opportunities, setbacks into stepping stones, and blunders into the pillars of a successful and satisfying life by accepting the lessons that mistakes provide.

Seeking Professional Help

There are times in life when the route ahead looks cloaked in doubt. Seeking professional guidance in these situations is analogous to discovering a guiding light that illuminates the path, providing clarity, knowledge, and a guaranteed path to success. It's an important and intelligent decision that can have a considerable influence on personal and professional development. Professional advisers are specialists in their industries, with extensive knowledge and experience. They have negotiated their domain's hurdles and complexities, making them essential sources of insight and guidance. Seeking expert assistance allows people to make more informed judgements. Professional advisers give insights that help you make confident decisions about financial, legal concerns, health, and other aspects of life.

Life is full with obstacles and difficulties. Professional advisers are skilled problem solvers, capable of analysing complicated challenges and suggesting answers that others may not see. Professional advisers can help you create a route to reach your goals, whether they be financial stability, a successful business, excellent health, or personal growth. They offer ideas and action plans that improve the chances of success. Professionals can assist in identifying and mitigating hazards. They protect against unforeseen setbacks by identifying probable dangers and developing contingency measures. Consulting with pros can help you save time and money. Their advice simplifies decision-making processes and reduces trial and error. Professional counsel is customised to your specific circumstances and objectives. Advisors consider your unique circumstances and preferences to ensure that the advice is relevant and helpful. Professional advisers may also provide emotional assistance in some circumstances. During tough times, they are a soothing presence, giving a secure environment to address concerns and fears.

Clients are often held accountable by professional advisers for their behaviour and aspirations. This accountability may be a strong motivator, propelling growth and achievement. Using professional advisers is a type of lifelong learning. It broadens your knowledge and abilities, promoting personal and professional development. A client's connection with their professional adviser is based on trust and confidence. Individuals may open up, seek assistance, and make key life decisions with confidence because of this foundation. Professional advisers frequently take a holistic approach, taking into account how different parts of life are interrelated. They assist folks with seeing the larger picture and developing tactics that are in line with overall well-being. Professional advisers frequently have wide networks and useful resources to offer their customers. They can put you in touch with other professionals or organisations that can help you achieve your goals. Seeking expert counsel can help you find clarity and success on your life's path. It demonstrates knowledge and a dedication to personal and professional development. Professional advisers act as guiding lights that help individuals to make educated decisions, achieve their goals, and ultimately find success and fulfilment, whether they are navigating the nuances of money, health, law, or any other subject.

CONCLUSION

The "Friday Harvest" stands as a tremendous crescendo of wealth-building through weekly possibilities in the big symphony of life, where the notes of opportunity and aspiration resonate together. As we get to the end of this exciting and enlightening voyage, it's evident that mastering the art of weekly options trading is a complex orchestration of knowledge, strategy, and caution.

The Friday Harvest is the product of hard work, smart preparation, and solid decision-making. It's a monument to the fortitude and endurance of individuals who enter into the world of weekly options, where each week gives a fresh opportunity to sow the seeds of financial success.

Individuals who participate in the Friday Harvest have the ability to design their financial destiny in the same way that a composer crafts each note and a conductor conducts the orchestra to perfection. They construct a symphony of wealth that resonates with their aims and desires via diversification, asset allocation, and attentive management.

Individuals participating in Friday Harvests prepare themselves with the knowledge and abilities to negotiate the market's unexpected rhythms by learning from mistakes, seeking expert assistance, and adopting risk management. They recognise that in the world of financial composition, adaptability, innovation, and growth are critical.

The Friday Harvest, with its weekly possibilities, is about developing a harmonious financial composition that matches with personal and professional goals, not merely money creation. It's a song of perseverance, wisdom, and resolve, performed with precision and driven by a desire for a brighter future.

As the last notes of our voyage fade into the distance, it becomes evident that the Friday

Harvest is a continuous symphony, a continuing pursuit of financial success, and a dedication to creating wealth week by week. In the vast symphony of financial progress, it is a celebration of the power of information, the art of strategy, and the tenacity of the human spirit. May your Friday Harvest be as abundant as your hard work and devotion allow, and may it bring you the finest songs of success and fulfilment.